LifeGuide® FAMILY Bible Studies

for Parents and Kids to Do Together

Grown Up on the Inside

18 Studies on Christian Character

With Notes for Parents

Jeffrey and Deborah Keiser

General Editor
James C. Galvin, Ed.D.

InterVarsity Press
Downers Grove, Illinois 60515, USA

Crossway Books
Leicester, UK

InterVarsity Press
P.O. Box 1400, Downers Grove, IL 60515, USA

Crossway Books
38 De Montfort Street, Leicester LE1 7GP, UK

InterVarsity Press®, U.S.A., is the book-publishing division of InterVarsity Christian Fellowship®, a student movement active on campus at hundreds of universities, colleges and schools of nursing in the United States of America, and a member movement of the International Fellowship of Evangelical Students. For information about local and regional activities, write Public Relations Dept., InterVarsity Christian Fellowship, 6400 Schroeder Rd., P.O. Box 7895, Madison, WI 53707-7895.

LifeGuide®is a registered trademark of InterVarsity Christian Fellowship.

All Scripture quotations are from the International Children's Bible, New Century Version, *copyright © 1986, 1988, 1994 by Word Publishing, Dallas, Texas 75039. Used by permission.*

This book was developed exclusively for InterVarsity Press by The Livingstone Corporation. James C. Galvin, Daryl J. Lucas and Linda R. Joiner, project staff.

Cover photograph: Michael Goss

Activities: Deborah Peska-Keiser

USA ISBN 0-8308-1112-5
UK ISBN 1-85684-131-6

Printed in the United States of America ∞

26 25 24 23 22 21 20 19 18 17 16 15 14 13 12 11 10 9 8 7 6 5 4 3 2 1

18 17 16 15 14 13 12 11 10 09 08 07 06 05 04 03 02 01 00 99 98 97 96 95

CONTENTS

CONTENTS

Welcome to LifeGuide® Family Bible Studies

If you have ever wondered how to make Bible study fun for kids, you will be delighted with this series of study guides. It provides an easy way to study the Bible with a young child or all together as a family. LifeGuide® Family Bible Studies were created especially for families with children ages 4-12. The simple, friendly format makes it easy for adults and children to finish together in just fifteen minutes a day. The material is undated so you can work through the guide at your own pace and according to your family's schedule.

Getting the Most from LifeGuide® Family Bible Studies

Understanding the format used in this series allows you to adapt each lesson to the needs of your family. Each lesson includes a passage from the Bible to read together, questions to discuss, fun activities and a prayer. You can spend more time on some sections and less on others, depending on the age and needs of your child.

Opening. When you sit down together, you need some way to focus your child's attention. The introductory paragraphs start with the child's frame of reference and leads him or her to the truth presented in the Bible passage. Often, the opening includes a question to ask your child or family so that you can find out more about what they are thinking. The opening also creates interest in the Bible verses for that lesson. If your child can read, have him or her read both the opening and the Bible text.

Bible Reading. The translation used in these study guides is the *International Children's Bible*. Having the text reprinted in the study guides makes it easy to use, and also allows children to use highlighters and colored pencils in their study of the Scriptures without fear of ruining a Bible. If you prefer, you can easily use other Bibles in conjunction with the lesson. Either way, the Bible reading usually generates questions.

Discussion Questions. Each lesson includes several questions to discuss to deepen your understanding of the passage. Some of the questions will require your child to look for the answers in the Bible reading. Others will help your child to think about how the truths apply to life.

✎More difficult questions for older children are marked with a pencil.

Activity. Each study guide contains a variety of fun paper and pencil activities such as simple crossword puzzles, mazes and decoding games. These activities can help motivate kids to complete the lesson each day. If you are sharing one study guide with several children, you can take turns letting each child complete the puzzle for the day.

Prayer. The main point of the lesson is also expressed in the prayer that you and your child can pray

Prayer. The main point of the lesson is also expressed in the prayer that you and your child can pray together. You can add more to each prayer as appropriate. But your child may not want to stop there.

Bonus. We have also included an active learning experience for a longer session when you have time and your child wants to do more. Or, you may want to save it for another day. The bonus activity provides additional reinforcement for the main point of the lesson.

Notes to Parents. You will find notes conveniently placed in the margins of each lesson rather than in a separate leader's guide. These notes provide practical help as you study the Bible together.

Studying the Bible with Children

You will find it useful to keep developmental differences in mind as you study the Bible together. After all, children are not miniature adults, and they would not learn well from Bible study approaches suitable for adults. The following chart illustrates some of the characteristics of children at different ages and relates them to Bible study. Which have you noticed in your own child?

Ages	Characteristics of Children	Implications for Bible Study
4-5 early childhood	In general, children this age: • learn by asking questions • usually have many fears • sometimes confuse make-believe with reality • have a growing sense of right and wrong • have a relatively short attention span (5-10 minutes)	As you teach your child: • allow them to ask questions, and answer them patiently • discuss God's protection • don't be surprised if Bible stories get mixed up with pretend stories • distinguish between right and wrong • don't expect to finish each lesson in one sitting
6-8 middle childhood	• are emergent readers; some are fluent readers • think concretely and literally; abstractions tend to be difficult • are able to memorize information easily • thrive on approval from their parents	• use this as an opportunity to practice reading skills • discuss the here and now, avoiding abstractions • make a game out of memorizing a few short verses from a study guide • praise and encourage as much as possible
9-11 later childhood	• are beginning to reason more logically • want to be independent learners • eagerly enter into competitive activities • have many questions about Christianity	• use the questions marked with a pencil, which are more challenging to answer • let your child set the pace and read as you facilitate • try not to have a winner and loser of the Bible study • help your child find answers to his or her questions in the Bible

With so many differences between older and younger children, you will have to adapt some lessons and skip certain activities. You may want to encourage the older children to help the younger ones. Think of these lessons as a helpful guide. Answering your child's questions may ultimately be more important than finishing a lesson. The following guidelines will help you adapt the lessons to meet the needs of children of different ages.

Using These Studies as a Family

You can use these studies to guide your family devotions. If you do, the biggest challenge will be keeping the attention and interest of both younger and older children at the same time. One useful technique for leading the discussion is to ask the question, then allow the children to answer one at a time, starting with the youngest and moving in order to the oldest. This way the younger children have a chance to talk, and the older children have a chance to add their answers. Don't let one child be critical of another child's answer. Parents can join in the fun, too. Your children will be interested in the personal applications that you see in the lesson.

You may have to change some of the wording in the lessons. When using the prayer as a family, change the *me* and *my* to *us* and *our*. Also, you may not want to do the puzzle as a group. Above all, keep it fun. Try to end with a snack or treat of some kind. You may find that your family wants to work through the entire series.

Using These Studies with a Younger Child

Younger children have boundless energy and short attention spans. Keep each lesson short and sweet. You may not be able to finish every lesson in one sitting; if so, just finish up the next day. Make use of the bonus activities at the end because these are more active in nature.

In general, don't use the questions marked with a pencil.

Some of the puzzles are designed to appeal to younger children, and some to older children. Feel free to skip the puzzles that seem too difficult.

Allow your child to ask questions at any point in the lesson. Sometimes the questions may seem endless, but that is a sign that your child is learning. Praise and encourage your child as much as possible during the study.

If your child cannot read, read the prayer one phrase at a time and have the child repeat it after you. Encourage your child to express his or her feelings to God in prayer, and also to make requests to his or her Heavenly Father.

If your child is an emergent reader, make the Bible study a fun experience by letting him or her circle important words or use a highlighter (just like Mom and Dad). Colored pens and pencils can add excitement to the lesson. Make Bible study an adventure.

Using These Studies with an Older Child

Older children don't want to be treated like little kids. They will quickly spot the parts of each lesson intended for younger children. If this happens, don't argue. Simply let them know that they will be treated differently, that they don't have to do all the parts of every lesson, and that this study should be very *easy* for them to complete.

In general, skip the bonus activities, because these are primarily for younger children. You can let your child choose whether or not to complete the puzzle in each lesson. Some of them will be far too easy, and some will be a challenge. The discussion questions marked with a pencil are more difficult and are for older children. Don't skip these. You may want to keep a concordance and Bible dictionary handy for questions that come up along the way.

Older children can be challenged to begin a personal devotional life. If appropriate for your child, consider letting him or her work alone on the study as a step toward developing a personal quiet time. Discuss the lesson with your child after he or she has answered all the questions.

The LifeGuide® Family Bible Studies

The entire series includes eight different study guides. Each study guide contains 18 lessons on a particular topic. Start with the topics that would be most interesting to your family.

Super Bible Heroes. The Bible is full of people who did great things, heroic things. But they really aren't very much bigger or stronger or braver than you. Reading their stories, you'll see how God can help you do what seems impossible on your own.

Grown Up on the Inside. Just as food, exercise and rest help us grow up on the outside, the Bible shows us how to grow up on the inside. It shows us how to practice being loyal, humble, honest, respectful and caring—everything that God knows will make us happy and healthy.

Fruit-Filled. Everybody has a favorite: blueberry Pop-Tarts, apple pie, Jell-O with bananas in it. The Bible tells us how we can be filled with God's favorite fruits: love, joy, peace, patience, kindness, goodness, faithfulness, gentleness and self-control.

Good Choice, Bad Choice. Every day we make choices: Will I watch TV or play outside after supper? What will I do when someone makes me mad? The Bible shows us how God helped other people make decisions—and how he will help us.

Jesus Loves Me. Jesus is the friend who never disappoints us or moves to another city. He is the friend who always understands our problems, who always has time to listen and help. The Bible shows us many ways Jesus loves us and helps us see his care in the things that happen to us every day.

The Friendship Factory. Friends make life fun. They help us learn, grow and know God better. And what the Bible says about friendship can help us be better friends to the people we know.

Wisdom Workshop. King Solomon wanted to be wise. So he asked God for wisdom. In the book of Proverbs he tells what God helped him learn about wisdom—and what you can learn too.

God's Great Invention. God made comets and colors and kangaroos. But his greatest invention is people—people like you. The Bible shows how God made you different from everyone else, with gifts and talents to make your own special mark on his world.

No matter which study guide you begin with, you will be introducing your child to the exciting challenge of studying God's Word and planting the seeds for a lifetime habit of personal Bible study.

James C. Galvin
General Editor

1

Becoming More Like Jesus

Most children can't wait to grow up. But being a grownup is not always fun. What do you think will be good about being a grownup? What do you think will be bad about being a grownup? *tennis player* *fun* *jobs*

All Christians start out like children spiritually. As we pray and read God's Word and worship with other Christians, we grow inside. Jesus taught his followers about growing up on the inside.

Allow your child to answer the questions. Commonly, children long for the privileges that older people enjoy. However, as they watch us labor, they may find adulthood somewhat ominous. Encourage him or her that, for Christians, being grown up on the inside is desirable for all of us.

Bible Reading

³[Jesus said] "Those people who know they have great spiritual needs are happy. The kingdom of heaven belongs to them.

⁴Those who are sad now are happy. God will comfort them.

⁵Those who are humble are happy. The earth will belong to them.

⁶Those who want to do right more than anything else are happy. God will fully satisfy them.

⁷Those who give mercy to others are happy. Mercy will be given to them.

⁸Those who are pure in their thinking are happy. They will be with God.

⁹Those who work to bring peace are happy. God will call them his sons.

¹⁰Those who are treated badly for doing good are happy. The kingdom of heaven belongs to them." (Matthew 5:3-10)

Discussion

1. Which of these verses is your favorite? Why?

vs. 7 because Alex thinks he has the gift of mercy

2. Why is it important for Christians to know that they have great spiritual needs and cannot do everything on their own (verse 3)?

3. What should we ask from God when we are sad (verse 4)?

4. How does Jesus want us to act around other (verses 5-7, 9)?

5. The passage makes it clear that this will make us happy. Use this opportunity to discuss the true happiness that Christ brings.

5. How does growing up on the inside make us feel?

6. The questions marked with a pencil are more difficult and intended for older children.

✎6. How can Christians be happy even when people are mean to them (verse 10)?

✎7. What does it mean to be pure in our thinking (verse 8)?

Activity

A B C D E F G H I J K L M N O

KINGDO<u>M</u>   HEAVE<u>N</u>

RI<u>G</u>HT   PE<u>A</u>CE

HUMB<u>L</u>E   COM<u>F</u>ORT

SAT<u>I</u>SFY   MER<u>C</u>Y

<u>H</u>APPY   PUR<u>E</u>

TREATE<u>D</u>   WOR<u>K</u>

<u>B</u>ELONG   G<u>O</u>D

Use the letters above to complete the words that are listed. Hint: All the words above appear in today's Bible reading.

Prayer

Dear Jesus,
Thank you for teaching me what it means to be grown up on the inside. I am glad that you promise to comfort me and be with me. Help me to become more grown up each day.
Amen.

Bonus

Ask your parent to help you find some pictures of yourself when you were much younger. Also, look through toys and clothes you may still have that you don't use anymore since you got bigger. Tell your parent what you remember about yourself when you were smaller. See if your parent can tell you any stories about yourself, too.

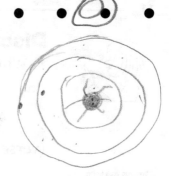

2

Growing in Bravery

Allow your child to answer the question.

Being brave is like being strong on the inside. It means doing what God wants even when you're scared. It is not always easy to be brave. When have you needed to be brave lately?

Moses was the leader of God's people when God rescued them from Egypt and led them through the desert. When Moses died, God needed a new leader to help the people move into the land God had promised to give them. There were many people to lead and many dangers ahead.

Bible Reading

⁶[The Lord said] "Joshua, be strong and brave! You must lead these people so they can take their land. This is the land I promised their fathers I would give them. ⁷Be strong and brave. Be sure to obey all the teachings my servant Moses gave you. If you follow them exactly, you will be successful in everything you do. ⁸Always remember what is written in the Book of the Teachings. Study it day and night. Then you will be sure to obey everything that is written there. If you do this, you will be wise and successful in everything. ⁹Remember that I commanded you to be strong and brave. So don't be afraid. The Lord your God will be with you everywhere you go." (Joshua 1:6-9)

Discussion

1. Who taught Joshua how to obey the Lord (verse 7)?

2. Why did Joshua need to study the Book of the Teachings (verse 8)?

2. You may want to tell your child that the Book of the Teachings refers to the books of Moses, the Pentateuch, which make up the first five books of our Old Testament.

3. What did God tell Joshua to help him not to be afraid (verse 9)?

4. What have you learned from God's Word that helps you to be strong and brave?

5. What will you do this week to help you remember and obey God's Word?

5. Help your child set a concrete goal, like reading a chapter of the Bible, memorizing a verse of Scripture, or learning a Scripture-based song.

✎6. Why will knowing and obeying God's Word make us successful (verse 7)?

✎7. Why do Christians need to keep studying the Bible?

Activity

The Lord your God will be
with you everywhere you go.

To find a promise from God in the Bible reading, rearrange the words
according to the symbols and write them in the blanks provided.

Prayer

Dear God,

Thank you for showing Joshua how to be strong and brave. Help me to be brave whenever I'm afraid to do what is right. Thank you for giving us the Bible. Help me to learn it well so I can grow strong on the inside.

In Jesus' name, amen.

Bonus

Joshua studied and obeyed the Ten Commandments. You can find these same commandments in the Bible. Ask your mom or dad to read them to you. They are in Exodus 20:1-23. See if you can memorize them by working on one each day.

3

Growing in Joy

Allow your child to answer the question.

Joy is a feeling of happiness on the inside. Joy makes you want to give thanks to God. When have you felt full of joy?

People who don't know God can't have joy that lasts very long. But being grown up on the inside means having more and more joy. Joy comes from knowing our God and all the wonderful things he has done. The more we know God, the more joy we will have. This psalm of David tells many reasons for Christians to be joyful.

Bible Reading

³Those who do right should be glad. They should rejoice before God. They should be happy and glad. ⁴Sing to God. Sing praises to his name. Prepare the way for him who rides through the desert. His name is the Lord. Rejoice before him. ⁵God is in his holy Temple. He is a father to orphans. He defends the widows. ⁶God gives the lonely a home. He leads prisoners out with joy. But those who turn against God will live in a dry land. (Psalm 68:3-6)

Discussion

1. How can God's people show their joy (verses 3-4)?

2. What reasons do Christians have for being joyful (verses 5-6)?

3. What does God give to those in need (verse 6)?

4. What keeps us from being more joyful?

5. What does God give that brings you joy?

7. Remind your child that joy runs deeper than surface emotions. The Psalms were used in corporate worship regardless of the circumstances in the lives of individuals. In the same way, the corporate worship we attend from week to week can be a means of acknowledging God's sovereignty even when we are feeling discouraged by the cares of the moment.

✎6. Why do God's people sometimes get discouraged and forget to rejoice?

✎7. When we are grown up on the inside, how can we rejoice even when we have troubles?

Activity

rejoice	Sing	joy	happy	to
God.	joy	Sing	praises	rides
to	holy	his	they	name.

Cross out the following.

1. Two words that begin with the letter *r*.

2. Two matching words beginning with the letter *j*.

3. Three words that end with the letter *y*.

When the squares that are left are read from left to right, you will find a message from the Bible.

Prayer

Dear God,
Thank you for giving me so many reasons to be joyful. I'm glad that you are the source of my joy. Please remind me to praise you and be glad about the things you give me.
In Jesus' name, amen.

When you finish with this activity, it might be a good opportunity to read Psalm 150 together. Talk about the difference between making noise and worshiping God.

Bonus

Create your own psalm or song of joy. Find any small instruments you own (including toy instruments) or make your own rhythm instruments. You can tap a plastic bowl or metal pan with a wooden spoon, seal some dry beans or rice inside a plastic container and shake it, or tap two sticks together. Then play your instruments as you sing a song of praise you know or say out loud, "Praise the Lord!"

4

Growing in Obedience

Allow your child to answer the question. Children may talk about times when adults ask them to interrupt something they are enjoying to do something else. Or they may focus on times when they are unsure of their own knowledge, strength or ability for doing what they are told.

Most children want to obey their parents. But no children are able to obey them all the time. When is it difficult for you to obey your parents?

Just like it isn't always easy to obey our parents, it isn't always easy to obey God. Some of God's special servants have been afraid when God asked them to do something difficult. Jeremiah, for example, once said he was too young to do what God asked. But obeying God helps us to grow up on the inside.

Bible Reading

[4]The Lord spoke these words to [Jeremiah]: [5]"Before I made you in your mother's womb, I chose you. Before you were born, I set you apart for a special work. I appointed you as a prophet to the nations." [6]Then I said, "But Lord God, I don't know how to speak. I am only a boy." [7]But the Lord said to me, "Don't say, 'I am only a boy.' You must go everywhere that I send you. You must say everything I tell you to say. [8]Don't be afraid of anyone because I am with you. I will protect you," says the Lord. (Jeremiah 1:4-8)

Discussion

1. What special job did God have for Jeremiah (verse 5)?

2. Why did Jeremiah think he wouldn't be able to obey (verse 6)?

3. What did God say to Jeremiah to help him obey (verses 7-8)?

4. How does God help us to obey him?

5. What can you do the next time it seems too hard to obey God?

6. In Jeremiah 1:5, God indicates that he is at work creating a unique person from the moment of conception and before.

✎6. How does God show Jeremiah that he is important?

7. Note: Jeremiah was probably a teenager, not a child like Samuel (1 Samuel 1:24-28) or the boy who gave Jesus his lunch (John 6:5-11).

✎7. Why doesn't God wait until we are grown up and confident before he calls us to obey him?

Activity

God wants us to ob*ey* him. Above are some other things that end in *ey*. Write what they are in the spaces provided underneath the pictures.

Prayer

Dear Lord,

Thank you for creating me and thinking about me even before I was born. I'm glad that you promised always to be with me. Help me to become more and more obedient to you as I grow. In Jesus' name, amen.

Bonus

Ask your parent to help you find a picture of yourself when you were a tiny baby. Sometimes it is hard to look at a picture like that and realize that it is really you! God knew who you would grow to be even *before* you were born. Take a piece of construction paper and lightly trace around the outside of the picture with a pencil (you can even leave the picture in a frame.) Ask your parent to help you cut a frame for your picture from the paper. Then decorate your frame and write the words *Created to Obey God* across the bottom. You can do this with a picture of your parent as a baby too!

● ● ● ● ● ● ● ● ● ● ● ● ● ● ●

5

Growing in Persistence

Allow your child to answer the question.

It is easy to give up. When have you felt like giving up? The opposite of giving up is persistence. It means staying with something until you reach your goal. God wants us to persist in doing right. God helped the people of Israel defeat their enemies in the city of Jericho, but only after they obeyed God for seven days in a row.

Bible Reading

²Then the Lord spoke to Joshua. He said, "Look, I have given you Jericho, its king and all its fighting men. ³March around the city with your army one time every day. Do this for six days. ⁴Have seven priests carry trumpets made from horns of male sheep. Tell them to march in front of the Holy Box. On the seventh day march around the city seven times. On that day tell the priests to blow the trumpets as they march. ⁵They will make one long blast on the trumpets. When you hear that sound, have all the people give a loud shout. Then the walls of the city will fall. And the people will go straight into the city." . . .

²⁰When the priests blew the trumpets, the people shouted. At the sound of the trumpets and the people's shout, the walls fell. And everyone ran straight into the city. So the Israelites defeated that city. (Joshua 6:2-5, 20)

Discussion

1. What did God tell Joshua and the Israelites to do (verses 3-4)?

2. What did God promise Joshua and the Israelites if they followed his instructions (verse 2)?

3. Why would it have been easy for the people to give up before the seventh day?

4. God had dried up the Jordan River so the people could cross into the land God had promised them. How would knowing this help them to keep going?

5. What good thing should you keep doing?

✎6. What should we do when obeying God looks silly to people who don't believe?

✎7. In what areas is it difficult for you to persist in doing good or obeying God?

4. The people Joshua was leading had also heard their parents talk about God's mighty acts. Reminding themselves of God's faithfulness in the past was a way of building their faith for the future.

6. Older children may have encountered questions from their friends about why they go to church, pray, avoid returning evil for evil, or follow other Christian practices. It may strengthen their resolve to understand that any act of faith makes more sense to those who have seen God's faithfulness over and over again. You might help your child devise a way to share about God with his or her skeptical friends. But most of all your child can see that what we know about God need not be shaken by the ignorance of others.

Activity

Joshua and his army were told to march around Jericho seven times and then blow the trumpets and *shout*. Find your way around the maze. Count each row as you go and take your turn to shout.

Prayer

Dear God,
Thank you for the Bible stories about people who didn't give up. Please help me to be more persistent.
In Jesus' name, amen.

Bonus

Act out the story of Joshua and Jericho. With some blocks or boxes, make an imaginary city of Jericho. Cardboard tubes or toy horns can be used as the trumpets. With a friend or someone else from your family, march around the city six times. The seventh time, sound the horns and shout.

6

Allow your child to answer the question.

Growing in Honesty

It is fun to play with friends who tell the truth and play fairly. God wants everyone to be honest. But sometimes people tell lies instead of the truth. How does it feel when someone lies to you?

The Bible says that people who are growing more honest will also be happier. Read these verses from Psalm 112 to find out how God feels about honesty.

Bible Reading

[1]Praise the Lord!
Happy is the person who fears the Lord. He loves what the Lord commands. [2]His descendants will be powerful in the land. The children of honest people will be blessed. [3]His house will be full of wealth and riches. His goodness will continue forever. [4]A light shines in the dark for honest people. It shines for those who are good and kind and merciful. [5]It is good to be kind and generous. Whoever is fair in his business [6]will never be defeated. A good person will be remembered from now on. (Psalm 112:1-6)

Discussion

1. Why do Christians want to be honest (verse 1)?

2. What is one way God can reward honest people (verses 2-3)?

2. Older children will be aware that at times there is a price to be paid for honesty. For instance, the person who admits to breaking a window will have to pay to replace it. Sometimes when we identify ourselves as Christians, we face discrimination. These consequences in the short term do not negate God's promises. By obeying God, we have the immediate blessing of a clear conscience. And God himself will bless us for being honest in his own way and his own time.

3. How do other people feel about a fair and honest person (verses 5-6)?

4. What else does God do for honest people (verses 5-8)?

5. What do you think is the greatest reward for being honest?

✎6. When is it most difficult for you to be honest?

✎7. What do you most want to remember about honesty?

Activity

SONERP   P E R S O N

RSFEA   F e a r

ANSDMOMC   c o m m a n d s

LPWERFUO   P o w e r f u l

IFMERLUC   m r s v f e v e

SEDSBLE   b l e s s e d

TEALHW   w e a l t h

CHRIES   r v e c h s

EHONST   H o n e s t

ONESGODS   g o o d n e s s

Unscramble the letters on the left to reveal words from today's Bible reading. When the blanks are filled in, a word will appear in the column down the middle that describes what we will be.

Prayer

Dear Lord,
Thank you for blessing honest people. Your Word teaches me that I will be happy if I learn to be honest. Please forgive me for the times I have not been honest with others.
In Jesus' name, amen.

Bonus

Play a game called "Guess What I See." Choose an object in the room and tell your parent what color it is. Give your parent five guesses. If your parent guesses right, be honest! Then switch and you guess the object. Then talk about how much more fun the game is when you are honest.

Growing in Hope

Allow your child to answer the question.

All of us have times when we feel afraid. Sometimes we are *so* afraid that it is hard to imagine that we will be all right. When have you felt afraid?

Sometimes God's people find themselves in scary situations. Even strong Christians can feel afraid. At those times, it is good to look at God's promises in the Bible. They can help us to be less afraid.

Bible Reading

[1]Now this is what the Lord says. He created you, people of Jacob. He formed you, people of Israel. He says, "Don't be afraid, because I have saved you. I have called you by name, and you are mine. [2]When you pass through the waters, I will be with you. When you cross rivers, you will not drown. When you walk through fire, you will not be burned. The flames will not hurt you. [3]This is because I, the Lord, am your God. I, the Holy One of Israel, am your Savior. [4]You are precious to me. I give you honor, and I love you. So I will give other people in your place. I will give other nations to save your life. [5]So don't be afraid. I am with you. I will gather your children from the east. I will gather you from the west." (Isaiah 43:1-5)

Discussion

1. What's the first thing God told his people to remember (verse 1)?

1. God created us—he would never abandon us.

2. When you are in a scary situation, how does it help to know that you belong to God (verse 1)?

3. What amazing protections does God promise to his people (verse 2)?

3. Be sure to explain to children that this verse uses figures of speech. They don't mean, "Go out and walk through fire." They mean, "When really tough things happen to you, God will be with you."

4. How does it feel when someone older and stronger tells you, "Don't be afraid"?

5. You might help your child focus on an upcoming challenge that seems frightening to him or her. As that time approaches, read Isaiah 43:1-5 together and pray together.

5. How can God's promises help you be hopeful this week?

✎6. Why is it comforting to know that God knows your name (verse 1)?

7. This might be an opportunity to help your child understand that trials build character. When we rely on the promises of God and see his deliverance, we build hope and confidence for the next difficult circumstance.

✎7. How can scary situations help us become more hopeful Christians?

Activity

Start here!

So __ __ __'__ __ __ __ __ __ __ __ __ __ __ .

__ a__ __ __ __ __ __ __ __ __ .

Start at the arrow and go twice around the figure eight. Write every other letter in the blanks. You will complete the sentence and discover a key phrase from the Bible reading.

Prayer

Dear Lord,
Thank you that you never forget about me. Help me to trust in your promises when I feel afraid. Thank you for promising to bring me through the scary situations in my life.
In Jesus' name, amen.

Bonus

Look through some old, unneeded magazines for a picture of a situation that looks dangerous or frightening. Cut it out and glue it to a large sheet of paper. Then think of a promise of God that would help you to have hope even if you found yourself there. Ask your parent to help you write a Bible verse under the picture.

8

Growing in Humility

Allow your child to answer the questions.

Before you go on with the study, explain to your child that the terms *Teacher, Father* and *Master* were used by the Jews of Jesus' time to mean "great one." He didn't want his followers to expect that kind of treatment from one another. He was addressing a competitive spirit among people who are all brothers and sisters in Christ.

Who is your teacher? your doctor? your pastor? One of the ways children show respect to grownups is by using a title in front of that person's name. Teachers, doctors and pastors do a lot of work to earn their title. We honor them by saying "Mrs." or "Dr." But it would be strange if you asked your friends to call *you* by a title! If you did that, you would need to show a little more *humility*.

It feels good to be honored by people. But if we think we are better than others and expect to be treated as important people, we are not acting grown up on the inside. Jesus was God's own Son, but he was humble. Jesus taught that true greatness comes from serving others. He wants us to learn to do the same.

Bible Reading

8[Jesus said] "You must not be called 'Teacher.' You are all brothers and sisters together. You have only one Teacher. 9And don't call any person on earth 'Father.' You have one Father. He is in heaven. 10And you should not be called 'Master.' You have only one Master, the Christ. 11He who serves you as a servant is the greatest among you. . . . 12Whoever makes himself humble will be made great." (Matthew 23:8-12)

Discussion

1. Who is the real Teacher and Father and Master (verses 8-10)?

2. Why doesn't God want us to think we are more important than other people?

3. How does a humble person get to be great (verse 12)?

4. What are some ways we can serve other Christians?

5. How can you humbly serve a friend or family member today?

✎6. Why is it a bad idea to look up to any one person too much?

✎7. Why is it sometimes difficult to serve others?

6. Excessive honoring of any human being is a problem not only for that person (spiritual pride) but for the Christians who might tend to look to that individual for direction when they should be looking to God and his Word instead.

7. Children probably have experiences that tell them that being a servant lacks glamor and often goes unnoticed or unappreciated. Help your child to see from this passage in Matthew that God notices the work of the servant and will honor him or her in ways more lasting than earthly appreciation.

Activity

B	R	O	T	H	E	R	S	S	M	H	C
F	C	F	E	A	R	L	I	E	G	E	H
M	A	M	A	K	E	S	S	R	O	A	R
A	L	T	C	T	E	T	T	V	D	V	I
S	L	L	H	Y	A	A	E	E	C	E	S
T	E	R	E	E	P	E	R	S	O	N	T
E	D	T	R	F	R	M	S	U	T	N	R
R	R	G	P	E	V	H	U	M	B	L	E

Find the following words from the Bible reading in the diagram above. Words may appear vertically, horizontally or diagonally.

CALLED   BROTHERS   PERSON   HEAVEN   SERVES   HUMBLE   CHRIST
TEACHER   SISTERS   FATHER   MASTER   MAKES   GREAT   ONE

Prayer

Dear Jesus,
Thank you for showing us how to be humble. Thank you for teaching us to live as brothers and sisters. Help me to grow more humble by remembering to serve others.
Amen.

Bonus

Make a "Servant Crown." Using construction paper or lightweight cardboard, cut out a crown. Decorate it with markers or crayons. Glue on glitter or foil stars if you have them. Then tape the ends together.

Tell your family that the Servant Crown is to be worn by the person who has a servant chore to do each evening—setting the table, washing the dishes, taking out the trash and so on. When you give the crown to the person who is serving, remind yourselves that in God's eyes the person who serves humbly is truly great.

Growing in Love

Allow your child to answer the questions.

Whom do you love? Who loves you? Love helps us get along with others. Sometimes it is not easy to get along with those we love! If we did not love one another, it would be very easy to stay angry and not to forgive. It would be easy to ignore people who need our help.

Jesus taught us to love each other. He also showed us how to love. He wants us to become more loving. Jesus told his friends that love is more than something we say. It is something we do.

Bible Reading

[16]This is how we know what real love is: Jesus gave his life for us. So we should give our lives for our brothers. [17]Suppose a believer is rich enough to have all that he needs. He sees his brother in Christ who is poor and does not have what he needs. What if the believer does not help the poor brother? Then the believer does not have God's love in his heart. [18]My children, our love should not be only words and talk. Our love must be true love. And we should show that love by what we do. (1 John 3:16-18)

Discussion

1. How do we know what real love is like (verse 16)?

2. What does it mean for Christians to "give our lives" for each other? (verse 16)

3. What is a loving thing to do with our money (verse 17)?

4. Why is it not enough to *say* we love somebody but not do anything about it (verse 18)?

4. You might want to encourage your child that there is nothing wrong with sincere verbal expressions of love. The problem is with words that are proven insincere when the person who says them is unwilling to follow through with action.

5. What can we do to have love in our hearts?

✎6. Why is sharing our things or our money an important way to show love?

✎7. What is one thing you can do to *show* your love to a friend or family member today?

Activity

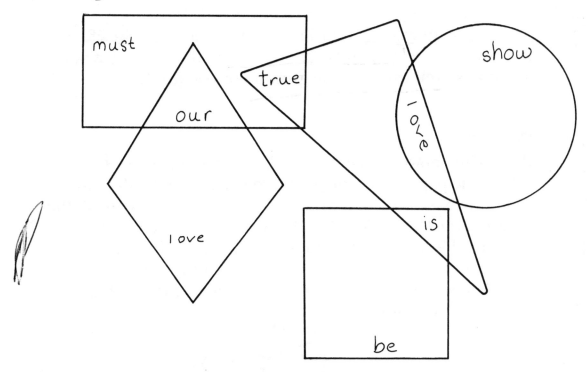

You will uncover a message to you from the Bible reading by answering the questions below and filling in the word.

our	love	must	be	true	love
What is in the diamond and in the rectangle?	What is not in the rectangle but is in the diamond?	What is in the rectangle but not in the triangle or the diamond?	What is in the square but not in the triangle?	What is in the triangle and in the rectangle?	What is not in the square but is in the triangle and the circle?

Prayer

Dear Jesus,
Thank you for *showing* your love for me by giving your life on the cross. Please help me to show love to others, not just talk about it, so you can help me grow up on the inside.
Amen.

Bonus

Draw a line down the center of a large piece of paper. On one side of the paper, ask your parent to write down all the ways you can think of to *say* "I love you." On the other side, write all the ways you can think of to *show* that you love another person. Then read Jesus' words again in 1 John 3:18: "My children, our love should not be only words and talk. Our love must be true love. And we should show that love by what we do." Which of the ways to show love could you do today?

10

Growing as a Servant

Allow your child to answer the question.

If you had a servant, what chores would you have that person do for you? Most of us like the idea of having someone else to do our work for us. We are not always as eager to be a servant for other people.

For Christians, an important way to grow up on the inside is to be willing to serve. God noticed a man named Joshua who had been serving Moses for a long time. Eventually God made Joshua the next leader of his people.

Bible Reading

[28]Since he was a young boy, Joshua had been Moses' assistant. (Numbers 11:28)

[13]So Moses and his helper Joshua set out. Moses went up Sinai, the mountain of God. (Exodus 24:13)

[18]So the Lord said to Moses, "Take Joshua son of Nun. My Spirit is in him. Put your hand on him. [19]Have him stand before Eleazar the priest and all the people. Then give him his orders as they watch. Let him share your honor. Then all the Israelites will obey him." (Numbers 27:18-19)

Discussion

1. When did Joshua start growing as a servant (Numbers 11:28)?

2. What person did Joshua follow and serve (Exodus 24:13)?

3. How did God tell Moses to honor Joshua (Numbers 27:18-19)?

4. What was Joshua's reward for serving Moses so well?

5. What are some ways of serving others that can help you to grow on the inside?

✎6. How did being Moses' assistant help Joshua get ready to lead the people?

✎7. How does serving others make a person a better leader?

1. Your child might be interested in other characters in the Bible who began their service to God at an early age, such as David, Josiah and Joash.

5. Help your child to see that his or her attitude about menial chores, even those which are assigned rather than chosen, can determine how much spiritual benefit results.

6. If you or someone you know is in the role of an assistant, give your child some concrete examples of the ups and downs of such a position.

Activity

Make a circle around the animals who are doing things to serve others. Write underneath the picture what they are doing to help.

Prayer

Dear God,

Thank you for giving us good examples in the Bible of people who served others well. Help me to better serve the people around me. Help me to serve you well. Help me to grow up on the inside.

In Jesus' name, amen.

Bonus

Find a way to serve your mom or dad tonight. You could set the table, help with the dishes or put things away. As you serve, think about Joshua and how he grew on the inside by serving Moses.

11

Growing in Forgiveness

Allow your child to answer the question. If your child brings up an incident that has not been resolved, be sure to help him or her to forgive. Your child may need to admit and feel the hurt or anger, or confront the person who hurt him or her (especially if the person was unaware of the damage done). Children should not think that forgiveness means pretending that their feelings don't matter.

When has it been hard for you to forgive someone who hurt you?

It is difficult to forgive when we are feeling hurt and angry. But the Bible teaches that growing up on the inside means learning to forgive others. Forgiving can make us happier because we let go of the sadness or anger. The best way to learn about forgiveness is to see how God forgives us.

Bible Reading

[4][Jesus taught us to pray, saying,] "Forgive us the sins we have done, because we forgive every person who has done wrong to us." (Luke 11:4)

[3][Jesus said] "If your brother sins, tell him he is wrong. But if he is sorry and stops sinning, forgive him. [4]If your brother sins against you seven times in one day, but he says that he is sorry each time, then forgive him." (Luke 17:3-4)

[13]Do not be angry with each other, but forgive each other. If someone does wrong to you, then forgive him. Forgive each other because the Lord forgave you. (Colossians 3:13)

Discussion

1. Jesus told us to forgive others. How do you feel when someone forgives you (Luke 11:4)?

2. Why is it good to tell your friends when they hurt your feelings (Luke 17:3)?

2. People are not always aware that they have done something wrong. Nor do they always perceive that their actions may have hurt another. The best way for them to learn is for a fellow Christian to call it to their attention. Then they have the opportunity to ask forgiveness of the injured parties and of God.

3. Why is it important to forgive someone more than just one time (Luke 17:4)?

✎4. Why is it really hard to forgive someone who has already hurt you before (Luke 17:3-4)?

5. Why is it important for Christians to forgive (Colossians 3:13)?

✎6. What are some things that would make you stay mad at someone (Colossians 3:13)?

7. Who is someone you will forgive today?

Activity

back	~~hun~~	~~br~~	~~bathro~~
pr	out	or	~~able~~

1. ~~bathrobe~~
2. ~~hungry~~
3. ~~brother~~
4. notable

5. ~~preach~~
6. ~~without~~
7. ~~back door~~

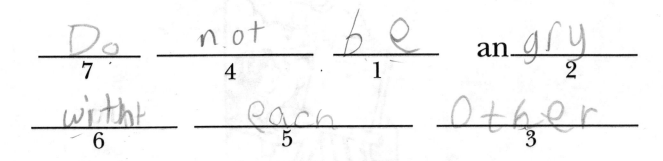

Do ___ n ot ___ b e ___ an gry ___
   7   4   1   2

witht ___ each ___ other ___
  6   5   3

Cross out the letters in the numbered words that match the letters in the boxes. Copy the smaller words that remain on the lines that have the same number. You will find a message from the Bible reading.

Prayer

Dear Lord,
Thank you for forgiving me when I have done wrong. Help me to forgive people who have hurt me. Help me to grow more forgiving on the inside.
In Jesus' name, amen.

Bonus

Draw a line down the center of a piece of paper. On one side, draw a picture of a time you did something to hurt a friend. On the other side, draw a picture of what happened when your friend forgave you. Then explain the picture to someone else.

12

Growing in Mercy

Allow your child to answer the questions.

Has anyone ever helped you when you got hurt? What happened? The person who helped you was showing mercy. When we show mercy, we are thinking more about how the hurting person feels than ourselves. A teacher of the law asked Jesus, "Who is my neighbor?" And Jesus told a story about a man who was hurt.

Bible Reading

³⁰Jesus said, "A man was going down the road from Jerusalem to Jericho. Some robbers attacked him. They tore off his clothes and beat him. Then they left him lying there, almost dead. ³¹It happened that a Jewish priest was going down that road. When the priest saw the man, he walked by on the other side of the road. ³²Next, a Levite came there. He went over and looked at the man. Then he walked by on the other side of the road. ³³Then a Samaritan traveling down the road came to where the hurt man was lying. He saw the man and felt very sorry for him. ³⁴The Samaritan went to him and poured olive oil and wine on his wounds and bandaged them. He put the hurt man on his own donkey and took him to an inn. At the inn, the Samaritan took care of him. ³⁵The next day, the Samaritan brought out two silver coins and gave them to the innkeeper. The Samaritan said,

'Take care of this man. If you spend more money on him, I will pay it back to you when I come again.' "

[36]Then Jesus said, "Which one of these three men do you think was a neighbor to the man who was attacked by robbers?" [37]The teacher of the law answered, "The one who helped him." Jesus said to him, "Go and do the same thing he did." (Luke 10:30-37)

Discussion

1. Why did the traveler need help (verse 30)?

2. What did the priest and the Levite do when they saw the hurt man (verses 31-32)?

3. What did the Samaritan do (verses 33-35)?

4. Why do you think the priest and the Levite decided not to help the hurt man?

✎5. Why do religious people sometimes fail to show mercy?

✎6. Why did the Samaritan take such good care of the man?

7. How can you show mercy to someone this week?

4. The priest and the Levite were obviously concerned about the cost to themselves if they got involved. Young children will probably understand that time and trouble would be involved in helping the injured man. Older children may be interested to know that these religious leaders knew that they would be ceremonially unclean if they touched the man. This would necessitate staying away from the temple for seven days and going through a detailed cleansing procedure.

6. The Samaritan was putting into practice the idea of doing for others what he would want someone to do for him in the same circumstances. It is clear from verse 33 that he was able to put himself in the man's place and feel sorry for him.

Activity

a b c d e f g h i j k l m n o p q r s t u v w x y z

Uifo   Kftvt   tbje,   "Xijdi   pof   pg

_____   _____   _____ ,   "_____   _____   _____

uiftf   uisff   nfo   ep   zpv   uijol   xbt

_____   _____   _____   _____   _____   _____   _____

b   ofjhicps   up   uif   nbo   xip   xbt

___   _____   _____   _____   _____   _____   _____

buubdlfe   cz   spccfst?"   Uif   ufbdifs

_____   _____   _____?"   _____   _____

pg   uif   mbx   botxfsfe,   "Uif   pof   xip

___   _____   _____   _____ ,   "_____   _____   _____

ifmqfe   ijn."   Kftvt   tbje   up   ijn,   "Hp

_____   ____."   _____   _____   ____   ____ ,   "_____

boe   ep   uif   tbnf   uijoh   if   eje."

_____   _____   _____   _____   _____   _____   _____?"

Use the alphabet to help you decode the paragraph above. Write the correct word in the space below the coded words. Hint: use the letter from the alphabet that comes before the letter provided.

Prayer

Dear Lord,
Thank you for the mercy you have shown to me by sending
Jesus to be my Savior. Please help me to be merciful to others
whenever I can.
Amen.

Bonus

Imagine what the hurt traveler would have wanted to say to the
Samaritan when he started to get well. Write a thank-you note
from the hurt man to the Samaritan (or ask your parent to
write your words). Or send a thank-you note to someone who
has helped you.

13

Allow your child to answer the question.

Growing More Generous

When have you really enjoyed giving a gift to someone? Sometimes you think and work hard to get just the right gift for a friend. If the friend is very excited to get the gift, you feel a special kind of happiness inside.

God wants his children to be generous. But he doesn't want us to give just because we have to. God wants us to give freely. That kind of giving makes you give happily. The person who gives happily is becoming more generous on the inside.

Paul wrote to the church in Corinth to encourage them to be more generous.

Bible Reading

[6]Remember this: The person who plants a little will have a small harvest. But the person who plants a lot will have a big harvest. [7]Each one should give, then, what he has decided in his heart to give. He should not give if it makes him sad. And he should not give if he thinks he is forced to give. God loves the person who gives happily. [8]And God can give you more blessings than you need. Then you will always have plenty of everything. You will have enough to give to every good work. (2 Corinthians 9:6-8)

Discussion

1. How is giving to other people like planting a garden (verse 6)?

2. When should we *not* give (verse 7)?

3. The ability to give cheerfully is evidence of an inner attitude of generosity. God desires not simply the outward manifestation but the inner maturity.

3. Why does God love the person who gives happily (verse 7)?

4. How can our giving bring praise to God (verses 12-13)?

5. To whom can you be generous? What can you give?

✎6. Why is it difficult for some people to be generous?

✎7. How does giving freely show we trust in Jesus?

Activity

Paul wrote:

$$\overline{}\ \overline{}\ \overline{}\ \overline{}\ \overline{}\ \overline{}\ \overline{}\ \overline{}\ \overline{}\ \overline{}\ \overline{}$$

3   8   1   10   8   16   9   12   5   4   9

15   9   13   12   8   14   2   4   8

3   6   16   9   12   4   11   15   15   6   10   7.

To complete the sentence above that was written by Paul, solve the problems below to find the missing letters.

O	D	V	G	E	S	T	R
5+3=	0+1=	8+8=	1+2=	5+4=	2+10=	4+1=	7+6=

H	P	W	I	A	Y	L	N
2+2=	12+3=	1+1=	2+4=	7+4=	4+3=	5+5=	3+11=

Prayer

Dear God,
Thank you for giving me the best gift of all, the gift of your Son, Jesus. I am glad that you taught me to be happy when I give. Please help me to become more and more generous on the inside.
In Jesus' name, amen.

Bonus

Think of something you would like to make for a friend or family member. (Not all gifts involve spending money.) Make sure it is something you can give happily. When your gift is ready, thank God that you are able to give this gift. Then give your gift. Tell God that you know he is pleased, and ask him to help you do more and more of this kind of giving.

14

Growing in Responsibility

At top right, partially visible: *2 Thessalonians 3:6–16*

A home runs better when everybody helps out. What chores do you do around the house to help your parents?

Everyone has work to do in order to live. People who live in families can share the work. But it would not be fair if one person did nothing and left the work for everyone else. That would not be responsible. The same is true in larger groups of Christians. Paul wrote a letter to the Thessalonians to tell them to each do their share of the work.

Allow your child to answer the question. If you don't have formal chores, chances are your child will perceive some of his or her activities as helpful, like hanging up clothing or putting away toys. After this lesson, consider choosing one or more new jobs that can be completed successfully by your child. This will help the child to practice responsibility.

Bible Reading

⁶Brothers, by the authority of our Lord Jesus Christ we command you to stay away from any believer who refuses to work. People who refuse to work are not following the teaching that we gave them. ⁷You yourselves know that you should live as we live. We were not lazy when we were with you. ⁸And when we ate another person's food, we always paid for it. We worked and worked so that we would not be a trouble to any of you. . . . ¹⁰We gave you this rule: "If anyone will not work, he will not eat."

¹¹We hear that some people in your group refuse to work. They do nothing. And they busy themselves in other people's lives. ¹²We command those people to work quietly and earn

their own food. In the Lord Jesus Christ we beg them to do this. [13]Brothers, never become tired of doing good.
(2 Thessalonians 3:6-8, 10-13)

Discussion

1. What did Paul tell the people to do about Christians who would not work (verse 6)?

2. How did Paul show Christians how to be responsible (verses 7-8)?

3. What should we think about when we get tired of working (verses 12-13)?

4. What does it mean for you to be more responsible?

5. What new job around the house could you choose to show your family you are growing in responsibility?

5. Help your child choose wisely so he or she can be both successful and helpful.

✎6. Why is it not good when people busy themselves in other people's lives?

✎7. How do we show love for one another when we work hard and learn responsibility?

Activity

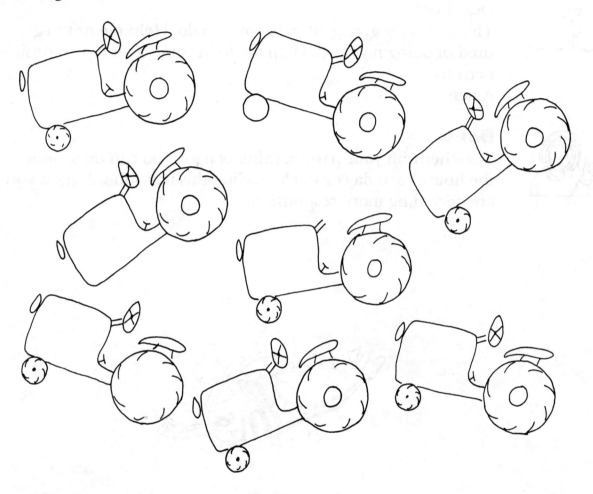

The tractor works hard for the farmer doing many different things on the farm. Like the tractor, we are to work hard. Search the tractors above to find two that are exactly alike.

Prayer

Dear Lord,
Thank you for giving all of us work to do. Help me not to get tired of doing my work. Help me to become a more responsible person.
Amen.

Bonus

Together with your parent, think of a job you can do around the house each day or week. Adding this new job will show you are becoming more responsible.

15

Growing in Unselfishness

Allow your child to answer the question.

Selfish people have few friends. But it's easy for most of us to be selfish. What does it mean to be selfish?

We know ourselves better than anyone else. It is easy to think about what we want so much that we forget what God wants. Paul taught that growing less selfish on the inside means asking God's Spirit to control our thinking. Then we can learn to please God and put others before ourselves.

Bible Reading

[5]Those who live following their sinful selves think only about things that their sinful selves want. But those who live following the Spirit are thinking about the things that the Spirit wants them to do. [6]If a person's thinking is controlled by his sinful self, then there is death. But if his thinking is controlled by the Spirit, then there is life and peace. [7]This is true because if a person's thinking is controlled by his sinful self, then he is against God. He refuses to obey God's law. . . . [8]Those people who are ruled by their sinful selves cannot please God.

[9]But you are not ruled by your sinful selves. You are ruled by the Spirit, if that Spirit of God really lives in you. (Romans 8:5-9)

Discussion

1. What does a growing Christian think about (verse 5)?

2. How do we experience life and peace when we let the Holy Spirit control us (verse 6)?

3. If we let our sinful selves control our thinking, what will happen (verses 7-8)?

4. Who is in charge of a Christian who is growing on the inside (verse 9)?

5. In what part of your life would you like to ask God to help you be less selfish?

✎6. How do we let the Spirit control our thinking (verse 6)?

✎7. Why is it hard to be a friend to a selfish person?

1. A growing Christian thinks about the things God wants him or her to do—serving others and showing love to them.

5. Help your child to think of areas where he or she repeatedly encounters selfishness. It may be with regard to toys or possessions, privileges within the family, time with parents or significant adults. Stop at this point and pray with your child to ask God's help in this specific area.

6. We let the Holy Spirit control our thinking by surrendering to him and by listening to what he says in his Word and accepting it as true and good for us.

Activity

What ends like *unselfish?*

cher	1. To make smooth	___ ___ ___ ish
f	2. A marine animal with five arms.	___ ___ ___ ___ ___ ish
pol	3. A language	___ ___ ___ ___ ish
fin	4. Lives in the water	___ ish
starf	5. To love something	___ ___ ___ ___ ish
fool	6. Something desired	___ ish
Engl	7. Being silly	___ ___ ___ ___ ish
w	8. To reach the end	___ ___ ___ ish

Use the definitions provided to reveal the words that end in *ish*. Extra help: Choose one of the letter combinations to the left to fill in the blanks.

Prayer

Dear Lord,
Thank you for the life and peace you give me when I let the Holy Spirit control me. Forgive me for the times I am still controlled by my sinful self. Help me to grow more unselfish every day.
In Jesus' name, amen.

Bonus

Draw a picture of a time when being selfish got you into trouble and made you unhappy. Explain the picture to your parent. Then draw a picture of a way you could act unselfishly. (Hint: Think of how you could share and give without concern for how much you get.) Then together ask God to help you to share and give unselfishly.

16

Growing in Wisdom

Allow your child to answer the question.

Truly wise people are not easy to find. Who do you think is a very wise person? Why?

Wise people don't make us feel bad when we have a problem. Instead, they are gentle and kind and try to help. As we grow on the inside, we can become wise people too. James, the brother of Jesus, wrote about the kind of wisdom God wants to see growing inside us.

Bible Reading

[13]Is there anyone among you who is truly wise and understanding? Then he should show his wisdom by living right. He should do good things without being proud. A wise person does not brag. [14]But if you are selfish and have bitter jealousy in your hearts, you have no reason to brag. Your bragging is a lie that hides the truth. That kind of "wisdom" does not come from God. [15]That "wisdom" comes from the world. It is not spiritual. It is from the devil. [16]Where there is jealousy and selfishness, there will be confusion and every kind of evil. [17]But the wisdom that comes from God is like this: First, it is pure. Then it is also peaceful, gentle, and easy to please. This wisdom is always ready to help those who are troubled and to do good for

others. This wisdom is always fair and honest. (James 3:13-17)

Discussion

1. How can we show that we are becoming truly wise (verse 13)?

2. Why does bragging show a lack of wisdom (verses 14-15)?

3. How do truly wise people act (verse 17)?

✎4. What does someone with fake wisdom want?

✎What does a person with true wisdom want?

5. James 3:17 gives us a way to measure whether we are growing in wisdom. Our attitudes and actions should reflect these virtues instead of producing jealousy and confusion.

5. How can you tell if you are growing in wisdom?

6. Why would the devil like to see more bragging, jealousy and selfishness?

7. What keeps us from growing in wisdom?

ctivity

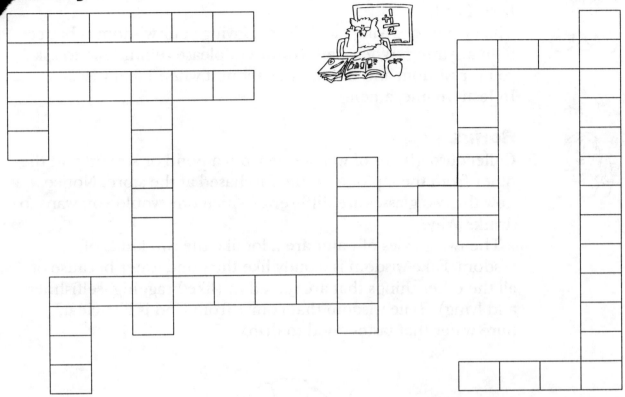

Below are some words from the Bible reading. Starting with the longest words, fill in the puzzle so that all the words fit.

4 LETTERS	5 LETTERS	6 LETTERS	7 LETTERS	9 LETTERS
pure	world	wisdom	trouble	spiritual
evil		reason		
brag		gentle	8 LETTERS	13 LETTERS
then			peaceful	understanding

Prayer

Dear Lord,
Thank you for giving us wisdom. Having your wisdom is better than anything. When I am confused, please remind me to ask you for wisdom and not to brag about it when I feel wise.
In Jesus' name, amen.

Bonus

Collect two glasses of water, one from a pond or stream and the other from the tap or a bottle purchased at the store. Notice how the two glasses are different. Which one would you want to drink? Why?

The two glasses of water are a lot like the two kinds of wisdom. Fake wisdom is cloudy like the pond water because of all the other things that are mixed in (like bragging, selfishness and lying). True wisdom that comes from God is like clear, pure water that tastes good to drink.

17

Allow your child to answer the question.

Growing in Respect

Being mean and poking fun shows a lack of respect for others. What are some ways to show respect?

Children are taught to respect their parents, teachers, pastors and other leaders because they are older and wiser. But God wants all Christians, even grownups, to be respectful. It is a way of showing that we believe that God is ruler over everything. When we learn to respect others, we are growing up on the inside.

Bible Reading

[13]Obey the people who have authority in this world. Do this for the Lord. Obey the king, who is the highest authority. [14]And obey the leaders who are sent by the king. They are sent to punish those who do wrong and to praise those who do right. [15]So when you do good, you stop foolish people from saying stupid things about you. This is what God wants. [16]Live as free men. But do not use your freedom as an excuse to do evil. Live as servants of God. [17]Show respect for all people. Love the brothers and sisters of God's family. Respect God. Honor the king. (1 Peter 2:13-17)

Discussion

1. How can we show respect for the people who lead us (verse 13)?

2. What important job do government leaders do (verse 14)?

3. What would people say about us if we were not obedient and respectful (verse 15)?

4. What are some ways that you can show respect for people (verse 17)?

5. How can you show respect for God (verse 17)?

✎6. How can Christians show respect to a leader who doesn't believe in God?

✎7. Why is it important for Christians to respect *all* people, even the ones who don't have authority over us?

4. Children may not yet identify common courtesies (like listening attentively, not interrupting, using polite greetings and remembering to say "thank you") as ways of showing respect. Help your child to set some concrete goals for applying this challenging teaching of respecting all people.

6. God has given authority to the people who rule over us. Unbelieving rulers can still help to keep the order God desires (see Romans 13). Even if the ruler is evil, we show our respect for God by being obedient. If obedience to God's law conflicts with obeying an earthly ruler, believers need to be prepared to take the consequences of their actions. The story of Shadrach, Meshach and Abednego in the Old Testament is a good illustration. By submitting to the king's consequences, they were still respectful, although they did not give in to the king and worship his idols. This story can be found in the book of Daniel, chapters 2 and 3.

Activity

 w 🐦 🔲 do good, 🔲 stop foolish 🫛 ple from saying stupid things about 🔲. This is what God wants. Live as free men. But do 🪢 use 🔲 r free-dom as an excuse 2 do evil. Live as seru🐛s of God. Show respect 4 all 🫛 ple.

This is 1 Peter 2:15-17 with pictures in place of some of the words. Without peeking on the other page, try to figure out what the symbols mean.

Prayer

Dear Lord,

Thank you for providing leaders to help keep order in our world. Help me to show that I believe in you by being obedient to those in authority over me. Help me to show respect for all people.

In Jesus' name, amen.

Bonus

Ask your parent to help you make a list of the people who hold authority where you live. Start with the officials in your town or city. Write down the name of the elected officials of your state or province.

Then read 1 Timothy 2:1-3 together. Use the list you made to pray for your leaders by name.

18

Growing in Holiness

Allow your child to answer the question.

Why do you think most people are afraid of the dark? Children are sometimes afraid of things in the dark that aren't even real. But even adults know that it would be easy to fall over something you couldn't see if you tried to walk in complete darkness.

The Bible uses light and darkness to describe holiness. Light is the opposite of darkness. Walking in the light means walking close to God. God is holy, and people who stay near him are becoming more holy. Read these verses from Ephesians where Paul talks about growing in holiness.

Bible Reading

[8]In the past you were full of darkness, but now you are full of light in the Lord. So live like children who belong to the light. [9]Light brings every kind of goodness, right living, and truth. [10]Try to learn what pleases the Lord. [11]Do not do the things that people in darkness do. That brings nothing good. But do good things to show that the things done in darkness are wrong. [12]It is shameful even to talk about what those people do in secret. [13]But the light makes all things easy to see. [14]And everything that is made easy to see can become light. (Ephesians 5:8-14)

Discussion

1. What does it mean to live in the light (verse 9)?

2. What does it mean to live in darkness (verse 11)?

3. Why do people do bad things secretly or in the darkness?

4. What kinds of actions and attitudes should we leave behind when we become children who belong to the light (verse 10)?

5. What kinds of things will we do when we live like children who belong to the light?

6. Paul is referring to the spiritual state of the Ephesians before and after they received Christ as their Savior. Only by God's grace and the saving work of Jesus Christ can people be rescued from spiritual darkness.

✎6. How do people who were full of darkness become full of light (verse 8)?

✎7. Why is darkness used to describe sinfulness and life apart from God?

Activity

mosqui	ed	clo	stop
lady	re	rry	sh

1. Sorry   5. belonged

2. relive   6. mosquito

3. ladylike   7. clothe

4. whosh   8. stoplight

Cross out the letters in the numbered words that match the letters in the boxes. Copy the smaller words that remain on the lines that have the same number. You will find a message from the Bible reading.

_____ _____ _____ children _____
   1   2   3   4

_____ _____ _____ _____.
   5   6   7   8

Prayer

Dear God,
Thank you for saving me and bringing me into the light of
Jesus. Help me to grow in holiness. Help me to walk in the light.
In Jesus' name, amen.

Bonus

Write a nice message to your parent in large print with a dark
crayon or marker. Then ask your parent to turn out all the
lights. (You may also need to close some drapes or a door so
the room is quite dark.) Hold up the message and ask your
parent to read it. Of course, he or she will be unable to read it.
Then turn on the light and share your message. Remember
that God wants us to live in the light and to grow in holiness.